Wildly Weird Weather

It's Raining Frogs!

By Jennifer Lombardo

Please visit our website, www.garethstevens.com. For a free color catalog of all our high-quality books, call toll free 1-800-542-2595 or fax 1-877-542-2596.

Cataloging-in-Publication Data

Names: Lombardo, Jennifer.
Title: It's raining frogs! / Jennifer Lombardo.
Description: New York : Gareth Stevens Publishing, 2024. | Series: Wildly weird weather | Includes glossary and index.
Identifiers: ISBN 9781538287941 (pbk.) | ISBN 9781538287958 (library bound) | ISBN 9781538287965 (ebook)
Subjects: LCSH: Tornadoes–Miscellanea–Juvenile literature. | Rain and rainfall–Miscellanea–Juvenile literature.
Classification: LCC QC955.2 L64 2024 | DDC 551.553–dc23

First Edition

Published in 2024 by
Gareth Stevens Publishing
2544 Clinton St.
Buffalo, NY 14224

Designer: Corinne Eberwine
Editor: Theresa Emminizer

Photo credits: Cover, Svoboda Pavel/Shutterstock.com; p. 5 Stone36/Shutterstock.com; p. 6 (graphic) VectorMine/Shutterstock.com; p. 9 Minerva Studio/Shutterstock.com; p. 10 Marek Mierzejewski/Shutterstock.com; p. 13 bradenjalexander/Shutterstock.com; p. 15 (frame) janniwet/Shutterstock.com; p. 15 (portrait) A.Sych/Shutterstock.com; p. 17 Konrad Lykosthenes/Wikimedia.com; p. 19 George Cruikshank/Wikimedia.com; p. 21 FloridaStock/Shutterstock.com.

Printed in the United States of America

CPSIA compliance information: Batch #CS24GS: For further information contact Gareth Stevens, New York, New York at 1-800-542-2595.

Contents

Regular Rain	4
The Water Cycle	6
Strong Weather	8
Light Frogs, Heavy Rain	10
What's It Like?	12
An Old Story	14
Frog Rains from History	16
Still a Mystery	18
Understanding Weather	20
Glossary	22
For More Information	23
Index	24

Words in the glossary appear in **bold** type the first time they are used in the text.

Regular Rain

We all know that rain comes from the sky, but do you know how it gets there? It might surprise you to learn that the water falling from the clouds came from the ground!

All of the water on Earth moves in a **cycle**. It goes from the ground to the sky and back to the ground again. Having a water cycle means that the same water is used over and over again. There's nowhere else to get it from!

Without the water cycle, nothing would be able to live on Earth.

The Water Cycle

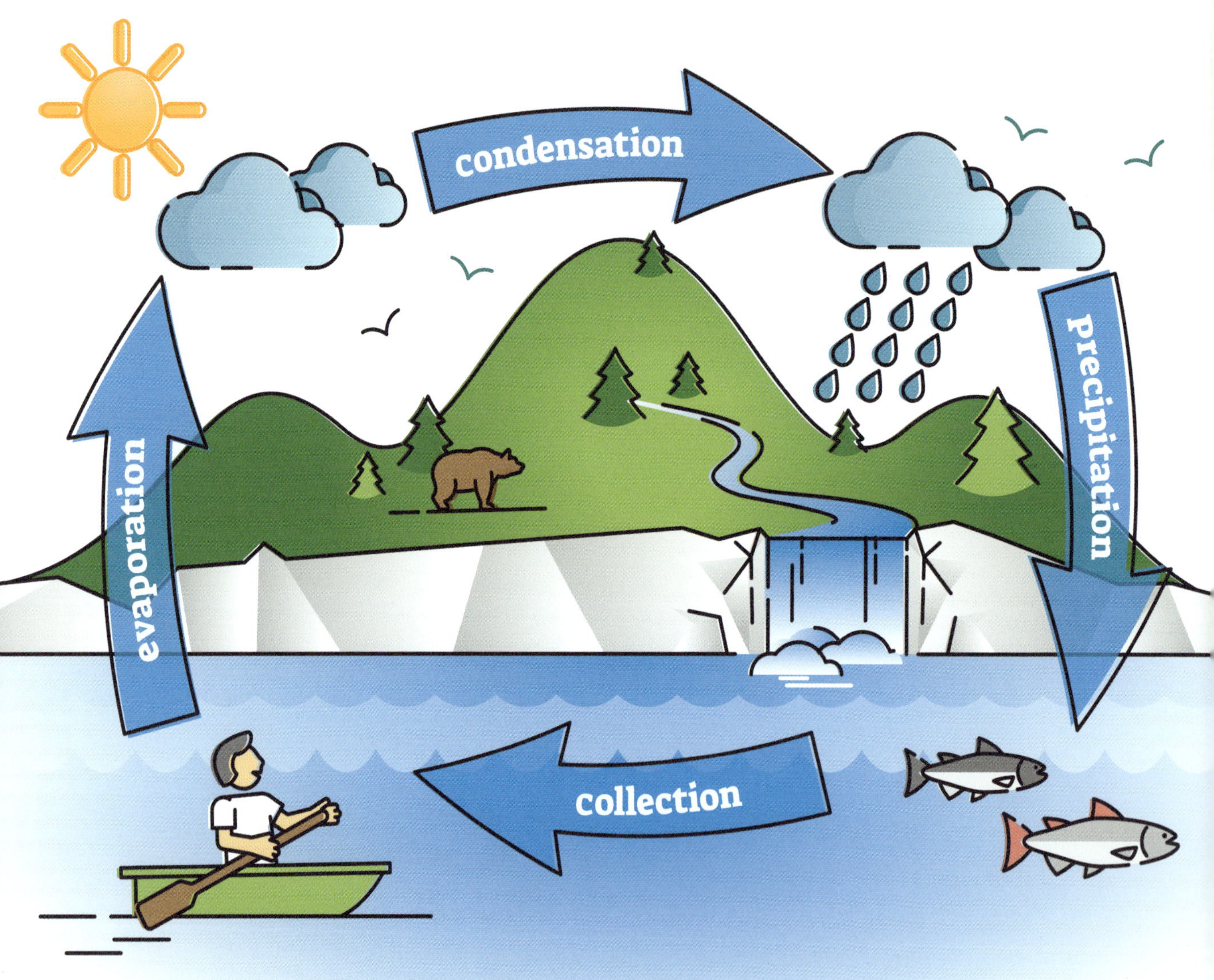

The sun heats the ground and bodies of water. It turns liquid water into a vapor, or gas, that rises into the air. This is called evaporation. In the air, it's cool enough to turn the vapor back into liquid water. This is called condensation.

The water condenses into clouds. When the clouds are too full, water falls back to Earth as rain, snow, or another kind of **precipitation**. This liquid collects in bodies of water or **soaks** into the ground.

This picture shows how the water cycle works.

Strong Weather

Sometimes water moves around in ways that aren't part of the normal water cycle. For example, a **tornado** that passes over water can pick that water up and drop it somewhere else. This kind of tornado is called a tornadic waterspout.

That's a Fact!

Some scientists believe any strong **updraft** can pick up frogs and carry them somewhere else—even if they're on land!

This picture shows a waterspout forming over the ocean. 

When a waterspout passes over a body of water that frogs live in, it can pick them up and carry them away. When the waterspout hits land, it dies down and drops the frogs, just like clouds drop rain!

Light Frogs, Heavy Rain

Frog rain doesn't happen very often, but it's more common than you might think. The winds that form a tornado are strong enough to pick up a car! Frogs weigh much less than a car, so it's easy for a tornadic waterspout to pick them up.

The *Sharknado* series of movies imagine what a tornadic waterspout of sharks would be like. However, scientists say sharks are too heavy to be picked up by a waterspout.

Other things get picked up with the frogs too. Fish, birds, and toads can all fall from the sky like rain when they get caught in a waterspout.

Frogs are very small and light, so they can be carried miles by a strong wind.

What's It Like?

You might be wondering what a rainstorm of frogs feels like. People who have been caught in one say it's **disgusting**! Air gets colder the farther up it moves. Remember—that's why condensation happens.

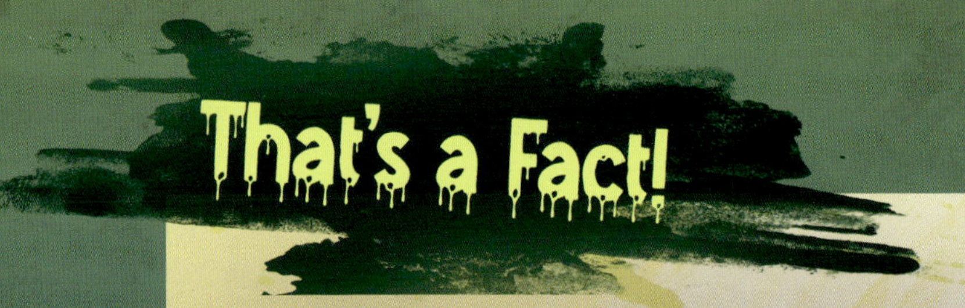

That's a Fact!

In 2005, it rained frogs in a small town in the European country of Serbia. Those frogs didn't die! People who lived in the town came outside to see hundreds of frogs hopping back to their ponds.

Air gets colder if a waterspout takes frogs high enough, they **freeze**. Imagine being hit on the head by a frozen frog! It wouldn't be much fun. Even if the frogs don't freeze, a lot of them die from falling back down to the ground.

Some frogs, such as this spring peeper, can ***survive*** *being frozen in a pond. It's unclear whether they can also survive being frozen in the air.*

An Old Story

Stories about a rain of frogs have been around for a long time. In the year 77, a man named Pliny the **Elder** wrote about them. He thought people were silly for saying that frogs rained from the sky. Instead, Pliny thought they grew out of the ground after it rained!

Since frogs do lay their eggs in water, Pliny's idea was closer to the truth about where frogs come from. However, he was wrong when he said that frogs could never fall like rain!

Pliny the Elder spent a lot of time thinking and writing about the world around him. He wasn't always right, but wrong guesses can lead to right ones later on.

Frog Rains from History

It doesn't rain frogs often, so people take notice when it does happen. For this reason, we have a lot of written **records** of this kind of weird weather. One rain of frogs happened in Kansas City, Missouri, in 1873. Another happened in Calgary, a city in Alberta, Canada, in 1921.

Frog rains can happen in any place where frogs live. In some places, other animals—such as lizards, worms, and crayfish—have fallen like rain in the same way.

This picture from 1557 shows frogs raining from the sky.

Still a Mystery

Even though scientists think they know why it sometimes rains animals, there are still some mysteries they haven't **solved**. One is why it often rains only one kind of animal at a time. If waterspouts are picking up animals from lakes, why doesn't it rain frogs and fish together?

Scientists don't have answers, but they have theories, or ideas. Some believe this has to do with how much the falling animals weigh. A storm loses strength over time, so it gets harder to hold onto objects.

During a heavy thunderstorm, people sometimes say it's "raining cats and dogs." However, there are no records of these animals falling during a storm like frogs and fish!

That's a Fact!

It makes sense that a storm would drop the heaviest animals first as it loses power. Then it would keep moving and drop lighter ones later. This means it could rain only fish in one town and only frogs in another.

Understanding Weather

Learning why it sometimes rains frogs helps us understand other kinds of weather better. Tracking a rain of frogs can show scientists how strong the winds are during a storm. It can also show them how far a storm can travel before it starts losing power.

Paying attention to the weather can help scientists see when it starts changing. The weather in a place over a long period of time is called its climate. When the climate changes, it **affects** everything around it!

Climate change can melt ice, cause worse storms, and harm plants and animals.

Glossary

affect: To create a change in something.

cycle: A sequence of events that repeats.

disgusting: Causing a strong feeling of dislike.

elder: Older.

freeze: To become a solid, such as ice, because of cold.

precipitation: Rain, snow, sleet, or hail.

record: An account of the way things happened.

soak: To enter or pass into something as a liquid.

solve: To find the answer.

survive: To live through something.

tornado: A storm of powerful winds that form a spinning tube of air.

updraft: An upward flow of air.

For More Information

Books

Farndon, John, Sean Callery, and Miranda Smith. *Weather.* New York, NY: Scholastic, 2020.

Finan, Catherine. *Weather.* Minneapolis, MN: Bearport Publishing, 2021.

Spalding, Maddie. *The Water Cycle.* Mankato, MN: The Child's World, 2019.

Websites

BrainPOP: Weather
www.brainpop.com/science/weather/weather
Watch a short movie and play games to learn more about weather.

Kiddle: Waterspout Facts for Kids
kids.kiddle.co/Waterspout
Learn more about waterspouts and check out some cool pictures.

Weather Wiz Kids
www.weatherwizkids.com
Read about all kinds of weather and do some fun science experiments.

Index

birds, 11
climate, 20, 21
clouds, 4, 7, 9
condensation, 7, 12
crayfish, 16
evaporation, 7
fish, 11, 18, 19
freezing, 13
frog eggs, 14
frog rain (examples), 12, 16
lakes, 18
lizards, 16
oceans, 9
Pliny the Elder, 14
ponds, 12, 13
scientists, 8, 11, 18, 20
Serbia, 12
sharks, 11
spring peepers, 13
storms, 12, 18, 19, 20, 21
theories, 14, 18
thunderstorms, 18
toads, 11
tornadoes, 8, 10
water cycle, 4, 6, 7, 8
waterspout, 8, 9, 10, 11, 13, 18
weather tracking, 20
weight, 10, 11, 18, 19
wind, 10, 11, 20
worms, 16